BUCKET

LIST

JOURNAL

This book belongs to

#1 :: ⭐

I want to do this because ....

....

To Make This Happen I Need to ....

....

Time Frame ☐ now ☐ soon ☐ by the age of ....

Date Completed .... Location ....

Solo / With ....

Story Behind It ....

....

....

....

What was the experience like

What I learned ....

....

....

Experience Rating ⭐ ⭐ ⭐ ⭐ ⭐

#2

....

....

I Want to do this because ....

....

To Make This Happen I Need to ....

....

Time Frame ☐ now ☐ soon ☐ by the age of ....

Date Completed .... Location ....

Solo / With ....

Story Behind It ....

....

....

....

What was the experience like

What I learned ....

....

....

Experience Rating ☆ ☆ ☆ ☆ ☆

#3

....

....

I Want to do this because ....

....

To Make This Happen I Need to ....

....

Time Frame ☐ now ☐ soon ☐ by the age of ....

Date Completed .... Location ....

Solo / With ....

Story Behind It ....

....

....

....

What was the experience like

What I learned ....

....

....

Experience Rating ⭐ ⭐ ⭐ ⭐ ⭐

#4

....

....

I Want to do this because ....

....

To Make This Happen I Need to ....

....

Time Frame ☐ now ☐ soon ☐ by the age of ....

Date Completed .... Location ....

Solo / With ....

Story Behind It ....

....

....

....

What was the experience like

What I learned ....

....

....

Experience Rating ⭐ ⭐ ⭐ ⭐ ⭐

#5

....

....

I Want to do this because ....

....

To Make This Happen I Need to ....

....

Time Frame ☐ now ☐ soon ☐ by the age of ....

Date Completed .... Location ....

Solo / With ....

Story Behind It ....

....

....

....

What was the experience like

What I learned ....

....

....

Experience Rating ⭐ ⭐ ⭐ ⭐ ⭐

#6

....

....

I Want to do this because ....

....

To Make This Happen I Need to ....

....

Time Frame ☐ now ☐ soon ☐ by the age of ....

Date Completed .... Location ....

Solo / With ....

Story Behind It ....

....

....

....

What was the experience like

What I learned ....

....

....

Experience Rating ⭐ ⭐ ⭐ ⭐ ⭐

#7

....

....

I want to do this because ....

....

To Make This Happen I Need to ....

....

Time Frame ☐ now ☐ soon ☐ by the age of ....

Date Completed .... Location ....

Solo / With ....

Story Behind It ....

....

....

....

What was the experience like

What I learned ....

....

....

Experience Rating ⭐ ⭐ ⭐ ⭐ ⭐

#8

....

....

I Want to do this because ....

....

To Make This Happen I Need to ....

....

Time Frame ☐ now ☐ soon ☐ by the age of ....

Date Completed .... Location ....

Solo / With ....

Story Behind It ....

....

....

....

What was the experience like

What I learned ....

....

....

Experience Rating ⭐ ⭐ ⭐ ⭐ ⭐

#9

....

....

I Want to do this because ....

....

To Make This Happen I Need to ....

....

Time Frame ☐ now ☐ soon ☐ by the age of ....

Date Completed .... Location ....

Solo / With ....

Story Behind It ....

....

....

....

What was the experience like

What I learned ....

....

....

Experience Rating ⭐ ⭐ ⭐ ⭐ ⭐

#10

....
....

I want to do this because ....
....

To Make This Happen I Need to ....
....

Time Frame ☐ now ☐ soon ☐ by the age of ....

Date Completed .... Location ....

Solo / With ....

Story Behind It ....
....
....
....

What was the experience like

What I learned ....
....
....

Experience Rating ⭐ ⭐ ⭐ ⭐ ⭐

#11

.... ⭐
....

I want to do this because ....
....

To Make This Happen I Need to ....
....

Time Frame ☐ now ☐ soon ☐ by the age of ....

Date Completed .... Location ....
Solo / With ....
Story Behind It ....
....
....
....

What was the experience like

What I learned ....
....
....

Experience Rating ⭐ ⭐ ⭐ ⭐ ⭐

#12 ....
....

I Want to do this because ....
....

To Make This Happen I Need to ....
....

Time Frame ☐ now ☐ soon ☐ by the age of ....

Date Completed .... Location ....
Solo / With ....
Story Behind It ....
....
....
....

What was the experience like

What I learned ....
....
....

Experience Rating ⭐ ⭐ ⭐ ⭐ ⭐

#13

....
....

I Want to do this because ....

....

To Make This Happen I Need to ....

....

Time Frame ☐ now ☐ soon ☐ by the age of ....

Date Completed .... Location ....

Solo / With ....

Story Behind It ....

....

....

....

What was the experience like

What I learned ....

....

....

Experience Rating ⭐ ⭐ ⭐ ⭐ ⭐

#14

....

....

I want to do this because ....

....

To Make This Happen I Need to ....

....

Time Frame ☐ now ☐ soon ☐ by the age of ....

Date Completed .... Location ....

Solo / With ....

Story Behind It ....

....

....

....

What was the experience like

What I learned ....

....

Experience Rating ★ ★ ★ ★ ★

#15 ....
....

I Want to do this because ....
....

To Make This Happen I Need to ....
....

Time Frame ☐ now ☐ soon ☐ by the age of ....

Date Completed .... Location ....
Solo / With ....
Story Behind It ....
....
....
....

What was the experience like

What I learned ....
....
....

Experience Rating ⭐ ⭐ ⭐ ⭐ ⭐

#16

....

....

I want to do this because ....

....

To Make This Happen I Need to ....

....

Time Frame ☐ now ☐ soon ☐ by the age of ....

Date Completed .... Location ....

Solo / With ....

Story Behind It ....

....

....

....

What was the experience like

What I learned ....

....

....

Experience Rating ⭐ ⭐ ⭐ ⭐ ⭐

#17

....

....

I Want to do this because ....

....

To Make This Happen I Need to ....

....

Time Frame ☐ now ☐ soon ☐ by the age of ....

Date Completed .... Location ....

Solo / With ....

Story Behind It ....

....

....

....

What was the experience like

What I learned ....

....

....

Experience Rating ☆ ☆ ☆ ☆ ☆

#18

....

....

I want to do this because ....

....

To Make This Happen I Need to ....

....

Time Frame ☐ now ☐ soon ☐ by the age of ....

Date Completed .... Location ....

Solo / With ....

Story Behind It ....

....

....

....

What was the experience like

What I learned ....

....

....

Experience Rating ⭐ ⭐ ⭐ ⭐ ⭐

#19 ....
....

I Want to do this because ....
....

To Make This Happen I Need to ....
....

Time Frame ☐ now ☐ soon ☐ by the age of ....

Date Completed .... Location ....

Solo / With ....

Story Behind It ....
....
....
....

What was the experience like

What I learned ....
....
....

Experience Rating ⭐ ⭐ ⭐ ⭐ ⭐

#20

....

....

I want to do this because ....

....

To Make This Happen I Need to ....

....

Time Frame ☐ now ☐ soon ☐ by the age of ....

Date Completed .... Location ....

Solo / With ....

Story Behind It ....

....

....

....

What was the experience like

What I learned ....

....

....

Experience Rating ⭐ ⭐ ⭐ ⭐ ⭐

#21

....

....

I Want to do this because ....

....

To Make This Happen I Need to ....

....

Time Frame ☐ now ☐ soon ☐ by the age of ....

Date Completed .... Location ....

Solo / With ....

Story Behind It ....

....

....

....

What was the experience like

What I learned ....

....

....

Experience Rating ⭐ ⭐ ⭐ ⭐ ⭐

#22

....

....

I want to do this because ....
....

To Make This Happen I Need to ....
....

Time Frame ☐ now ☐ soon ☐ by the age of ....

Date Completed .... Location ....
Solo / With ....
Story Behind It ....
....
....
....

What was the experience like

What I learned ....
....
....

Experience Rating ☆ ☆ ☆ ☆ ☆

#23 ....
....

I want to do this because ....
....

To Make This Happen I Need to ....
....

Time Frame ☐ now ☐ soon ☐ by the age of ....

Date Completed .... Location ....
Solo / With ....
Story Behind It ....
....
....
....

What was the experience like

What I learned ....
....
....

Experience Rating ⭐ ⭐ ⭐ ⭐ ⭐

#24

I want to do this because ....
....

To Make This Happen I Need to ....
....

Time Frame ☐ now ☐ soon ☐ by the age of ....

Date Completed .... Location ....
Solo / With ....
Story Behind It ....
....
....
....

What was the experience like

What I learned ....
....
....

Experience Rating ☆ ☆ ☆ ☆ ☆

#25 ....
....

I Want to do this because ....
....

To Make This Happen I Need to ....
....

Time Frame ☐ now ☐ soon ☐ by the age of ....

Date Completed .... Location ....
Solo / With ....
Story Behind It ....
....
....
....

What was the experience like

What I learned ....
....
....

Experience Rating ⭐ ⭐ ⭐ ⭐ ⭐

#26

....

....

I Want to do this because ....

....

To Make This Happen I Need to ....

....

Time Frame ☐ now ☐ soon ☐ by the age of ....

Date Completed .... Location ....

Solo / With ....

Story Behind It ....

....

....

....

What was the experience like

What I learned ....

....

....

Experience Rating ⭐ ⭐ ⭐ ⭐ ⭐

#27

....
....

I want to do this because ....
....

To Make This Happen I Need to ....
....

Time Frame ☐ now ☐ soon ☐ by the age of ....

Date Completed .... Location ....
Solo / With ....
Story Behind It ....
....
....
....

What was the experience like

What I learned ....
....
....

Experience Rating ⭐ ⭐ ⭐ ⭐ ⭐

#28

....

....

I Want to do this because ....

....

To Make This Happen I Need to ....

....

Time Frame ☐ now ☐ soon ☐ by the age of ....

Date Completed .... Location ....

Solo / With ....

Story Behind It ....

....

....

....

What was the experience like

What I learned ....

....

....

Experience Rating ⭐ ⭐ ⭐ ⭐ ⭐

#29

....

....

I want to do this because ....

....

To Make This Happen I Need to ....

....

Time Frame ☐ now ☐ soon ☐ by the age of ....

Date Completed .... Location ....

Solo / With ....

Story Behind It ....

....

....

....

What was the experience like

What I learned ....

....

....

Experience Rating ⭐ ⭐ ⭐ ⭐ ⭐

#30

....

....

I Want to do this because ....

....

To Make This Happen I Need to ....

....

Time Frame ☐ now ☐ soon ☐ by the age of ....

Date Completed .... Location ....

Solo / With ....

Story Behind It ....

....

....

....

What was the experience like

What I learned ....

....

....

Experience Rating ⭐ ⭐ ⭐ ⭐ ⭐

#31 ....
....

I want to do this because ....
....

To Make This Happen I Need to ....
....

Time Frame ☐ now ☐ soon ☐ by the age of ....

Date Completed .... Location ....
Solo / With ....
Story Behind It ....
....
....
....

What was the experience like

What I learned ....
....
....

Experience Rating ⭐ ⭐ ⭐ ⭐ ⭐

#32

....
....

I want to do this because ....
....

To Make This Happen I Need to ....
....

Time Frame ☐ now ☐ soon ☐ by the age of ....

Date Completed .... Location ....
Solo / With ....
Story Behind It ....
....
....
....

What was the experience like

What I learned ....
....
....

Experience Rating ⭐ ⭐ ⭐ ⭐ ⭐

#33

I Want to do this because ....

....

To Make This Happen I Need to ....

....

Time Frame ☐ now ☐ soon ☐ by the age of ....

Date Completed .... Location ....

Solo / With ....

Story Behind It ....

....

....

....

What was the experience like

What I learned ....

....

....

Experience Rating ⭐ ⭐ ⭐ ⭐ ⭐

#34

....

....

I Want to do this because ....

....

To Make This Happen I Need to ....

....

Time Frame ☐ now ☐ soon ☐ by the age of ....

Date Completed .... Location ....

Solo / With ....

Story Behind It ....

....

....

....

What was the experience like

What I learned ....

....

....

Experience Rating ⭐ ⭐ ⭐ ⭐ ⭐

#35 ....
....

I want to do this because ....
....

To Make This Happen I Need to ....
....

Time Frame ☐ now ☐ soon ☐ by the age of ....

Date Completed .... Location ....
Solo / With ....
Story Behind It ....
....
....
....

What was the experience like

What I learned ....
....
....

Experience Rating ⭐ ⭐ ⭐ ⭐ ⭐

#36

....
....

I Want to do this because ....
....

To Make This Happen I Need to ....
....

Time Frame ☐ now ☐ soon ☐ by the age of ....

Date Completed .... Location ....

Solo / With ....

Story Behind It ....
....
....
....

What was the experience like

What I learned ....
....
....

Experience Rating ⭐ ⭐ ⭐ ⭐ ⭐

#37 ....

I want to do this because ....
....

To Make This Happen I Need to ....
....

Time Frame ☐ now ☐ soon ☐ by the age of ....

Date Completed .... Location ....

Solo / With ....

Story Behind It ....
....
....
....

What was the experience like

What I learned ....
....
....

Experience Rating ⭐ ⭐ ⭐ ⭐ ⭐

#38 ....
....

I Want to do this because ....
....

To Make This Happen I Need to ....
....

Time Frame ☐ now ☐ soon ☐ by the age of ....

Date Completed .... Location ....
Solo / With ....
Story Behind It ....
....
....
....

What was the experience like

What I learned ....
....
....

Experience Rating ⭐ ⭐ ⭐ ⭐ ⭐

#39

....

....

I Want to do this because ....

....

To Make This Happen I Need to ....

....

Time Frame ☐ now ☐ soon ☐ by the age of ....

Date Completed .... Location ....

Solo / With ....

Story Behind It ....

....

....

....

What was the experience like

What I learned ....

....

....

Experience Rating ⭐ ⭐ ⭐ ⭐ ⭐

#40

....

....

I Want to do this because ....

....

To Make This Happen I Need to ....

....

Time Frame ☐ now ☐ soon ☐ by the age of ....

Date Completed .... Location ....

Solo / With ....

Story Behind It ....

....

....

....

What was the experience like

What I learned ....

....

....

Experience Rating ⭐ ⭐ ⭐ ⭐ ⭐

#41

....

....

I want to do this because ....

....

To Make This Happen I Need to ....

....

Time Frame ☐ now ☐ soon ☐ by the age of ....

Date Completed .... Location ....

Solo / With ....

Story Behind It ....

....

....

....

What was the experience like

What I learned ....

....

....

Experience Rating ⭐ ⭐ ⭐ ⭐ ⭐

#42

....

....

I Want to do this because ....

....

To Make This Happen I Need to ....

....

Time Frame ☐ now ☐ soon ☐ by the age of ....

Date Completed .... Location ....

Solo / With ....

Story Behind It ....

....

....

....

What was the experience like

What I learned ....

....

....

Experience Rating ⭐ ⭐ ⭐ ⭐ ⭐

#43

....

....

I want to do this because ....

....

To Make This Happen I Need to ....

....

Time Frame ☐ now ☐ soon ☐ by the age of ....

Date Completed .... Location ....

Solo / With ....

Story Behind It ....

....

....

....

What was the experience like

What I learned ....

....

....

Experience Rating ⭐ ⭐ ⭐ ⭐ ⭐

#44

I Want to do this because ....
....

To Make This Happen I Need to ....
....

Time Frame ☐ now ☐ soon ☐ by the age of ....

Date Completed .... Location ....
Solo / With ....
Story Behind It ....
....
....
....

What was the experience like

What I learned ....
....
....

Experience Rating ⭐ ⭐ ⭐ ⭐ ⭐

#45 ⋯⋯⋯⋯⋯⋯⋯⋯⋯⋯⋯

I Want to do this because ⋯⋯⋯⋯⋯⋯⋯⋯⋯⋯⋯⋯⋯⋯⋯⋯

To Make This Happen I Need to ⋯⋯⋯⋯⋯⋯⋯⋯⋯⋯

Time Frame ☐ now ☐ soon ☐ by the age of ⋯⋯⋯⋯

Date Completed ⋯⋯⋯⋯⋯⋯ Location ⋯⋯⋯⋯⋯⋯⋯

Solo / With ⋯⋯⋯⋯⋯⋯⋯⋯⋯⋯⋯⋯⋯⋯⋯⋯

Story Behind It ⋯⋯⋯⋯⋯⋯⋯⋯⋯⋯⋯⋯⋯⋯

⋯⋯⋯⋯⋯⋯⋯⋯⋯⋯⋯⋯⋯⋯⋯⋯⋯⋯⋯⋯

What was the experience like

What I learned ⋯⋯⋯⋯⋯⋯⋯⋯⋯⋯⋯⋯⋯

⋯⋯⋯⋯⋯⋯⋯⋯⋯⋯⋯⋯⋯⋯⋯⋯⋯⋯⋯⋯

Experience Rating ★ ★ ★ ★ ★

#46 ....
....

I Want to do this because ....
....

To Make This Happen I Need to ....
....

Time Frame ☐ now ☐ soon ☐ by the age of ....

Date Completed .... Location ....
Solo / With ....
Story Behind It ....
....
....
....

What was the experience like

What I learned ....
....
....

Experience Rating ⭐ ⭐ ⭐ ⭐ ⭐

#47 ....
....

I Want to do this because ....

....

To Make This Happen I Need to ....

....

Time Frame ☐ now ☐ soon ☐ by the age of ....

Date Completed .... Location ....

Solo / With ....

Story Behind It ....

....

....

....

What was the experience like

What I learned ....

....

....

Experience Rating ⭐ ⭐ ⭐ ⭐

#48

....

....

I want to do this because ....

....

To Make This Happen I Need to ....

....

Time Frame ☐ now ☐ soon ☐ by the age of ....

Date Completed .... Location ....

Solo / With ....

Story Behind It ....

....

....

....

What was the experience like

What I learned ....

....

....

Experience Rating ⭐ ⭐ ⭐ ⭐ ⭐

#49

....

....

I Want to do this because ....

....

To Make This Happen I Need to ....

....

Time Frame ☐ now ☐ soon ☐ by the age of ....

Date Completed .... Location ....

Solo / With ....

Story Behind It ....

....

....

....

What was the experience like

What I learned ....

....

....

Experience Rating ⭐ ⭐ ⭐ ⭐ ⭐

#50

....

....

I want to do this because ....

....

To Make This Happen I Need to ....

....

Time Frame ☐ now ☐ soon ☐ by the age of ....

Date Completed .... Location ....

Solo / With ....

Story Behind It ....

....

....

....

What was the experience like

What I learned ....

....

....

Experience Rating ⭐ ⭐ ⭐ ⭐ ⭐

#51

....

....

I Want to do this because ....

....

To Make This Happen I Need to ....

....

Time Frame ☐ now ☐ soon ☐ by the age of ....

Date Completed .... Location ....

Solo / With ....

Story Behind It ....

....

....

....

What was the experience like

What I learned ....

....

....

Experience Rating ⭐ ⭐ ⭐ ⭐ ⭐

#52 ....
....

I Want to do this because ....
....

To Make This Happen I Need to ....
....

Time Frame ☐ now ☐ soon ☐ by the age of ....

Date Completed .... Location ....
Solo / With ....
Story Behind It ....
....
....
....

What was the experience like

What I learned ....
....
....

Experience Rating ⭐ ⭐ ⭐ ⭐ ⭐

#53

....

....

I want to do this because ....

....

To Make This Happen I Need to ....

....

Time Frame ☐ now ☐ soon ☐ by the age of ....

Date Completed .... Location ....

Solo / With ....

Story Behind It ....

....

....

....

What was the experience like

What I learned ....

....

Experience Rating ⭐ ⭐ ⭐ ⭐ ⭐

#54

....

....

I Want to do this because ....

....

To Make This Happen I Need to ....

....

Time Frame ☐ now ☐ soon ☐ by the age of ....

Date Completed .... Location ....

Solo / With ....

Story Behind It ....

....

....

....

What was the experience like

What I learned ....

....

....

Experience Rating ⭐ ⭐ ⭐ ⭐ ⭐

#55

....

I Want to do this because ....

....

To Make This Happen I Need to ....

....

Time Frame ☐ now ☐ soon ☐ by the age of ....

Date Completed .... Location ....

Solo / With ....

Story Behind It ....

....

....

....

What was the experience like

What I learned ....

....

....

Experience Rating ⭐ ⭐ ⭐ ⭐ ⭐

#56

....

....

I Want to do this because ....

....

To Make This Happen I Need to ....

....

Time Frame ☐ now ☐ soon ☐ by the age of ....

Date Completed .... Location ....

Solo / With ....

Story Behind It ....

....

....

....

What was the experience like

What I learned ....

....

....

Experience Rating ⭐ ⭐ ⭐ ⭐ ⭐

#57 ....
....

I Want to do this because ....
....

To Make This Happen I Need to ....
....

Time Frame ☐ now ☐ soon ☐ by the age of ....

Date Completed .... Location ....

Solo / With ....

Story Behind It ....
....
....
....

What was the experience like

What I learned ....
....
....

Experience Rating ⭐ ⭐ ⭐ ⭐ ⭐

#58

....

....

I Want to do this because ....

....

To Make This Happen I Need to ....

....

Time Frame ☐ now ☐ soon ☐ by the age of ....

Date Completed .... Location ....

Solo / With ....

Story Behind It ....

....

....

....

What was the experience like

What I learned ....

....

....

Experience Rating ☆ ☆ ☆ ☆ ☆

#59

....
....

I Want to do this because ....
....

To Make This Happen I Need to ....
....

Time Frame ☐ now ☐ soon ☐ by the age of ....

Date Completed .... Location ....
Solo / With ....
Story Behind It ....
....
....
....

What was the experience like

What I learned ....
....
....

Experience Rating ⭐ ⭐ ⭐ ⭐ ⭐

#60

....

....

I want to do this because ....

....

To Make This Happen I Need to ....

....

Time Frame ☐ now ☐ soon ☐ by the age of ....

Date Completed .... Location ....

Solo / With ....

Story Behind It ....

....

....

....

What was the experience like

What I learned ....

....

....

Experience Rating ⭐ ⭐ ⭐ ⭐ ⭐

#61 ....
....

I Want to do this because ....
....

To Make This Happen I Need to ....
....

Time Frame ☐ now ☐ soon ☐ by the age of ....

Date Completed .... Location ....
Solo / With ....
Story Behind It ....
....
....
....

What was the experience like

What I learned ....
....
....

Experience Rating ⭐ ⭐ ⭐ ⭐ ⭐

#62

....

....

I Want to do this because ....

....

To Make This Happen I Need to ....

....

Time Frame ☐ now ☐ soon ☐ by the age of ....

Date Completed .... Location ....

Solo / With ....

Story Behind It ....

....

....

....

What was the experience like

What I learned ....

....

....

Experience Rating ⭐ ⭐ ⭐ ⭐ ⭐

#63 ·································
·································

I want to do this because ···································
··

To Make This Happen I Need to ··························
··

Time Frame ☐ now ☐ soon ☐ by the age of ············

Date Completed ···················· Location ···················
Solo / With ···
Story Behind It ···
··
··
··

What was the experience like

What I learned ···
··
··

Experience Rating ⭐ ⭐ ⭐ ⭐ ⭐

#64

....

....

I Want to do this because ....

....

To Make This Happen I Need to ....

....

Time Frame ☐ now ☐ soon ☐ by the age of ....

Date Completed .... Location ....

Solo / With ....

Story Behind It ....

....

....

....

What was the experience like

What I learned ....

....

....

Experience Rating ⭐ ⭐ ⭐ ⭐ ⭐

#65 ....

I want to do this because ....
....

To Make This Happen I Need to ....
....

Time Frame ☐ now ☐ soon ☐ by the age of ....

Date Completed .... Location ....
Solo / With ....
Story Behind It ....
....
....
....

What was the experience like

What I learned ....
....
....

Experience Rating ⭐ ⭐ ⭐ ⭐ ⭐

#66 ....
....

I want to do this because ....
....

To Make This Happen I Need to ....
....

Time Frame ☐ now ☐ soon ☐ by the age of ....

Date Completed .... Location ....
Solo / With ....
Story Behind It ....
....
....
....

What was the experience like

What I learned ....
....
....

Experience Rating ☆ ☆ ☆ ☆ ☆

#67

··

I want to do this because ··

··

To Make This Happen I Need to ··

··

Time Frame ☐ now ☐ soon ☐ by the age of ·············

Date Completed ························ Location ························

Solo / With ··

Story Behind It ··

··

··

··

What was the experience like

What I learned ··

··

··

Experience Rating ⭐ ⭐ ⭐ ⭐ ⭐

#68

....

....

I Want to do this because ....

....

To Make This Happen I Need to ....

....

Time Frame ☐ now ☐ soon ☐ by the age of ....

Date Completed .... Location ....

Solo / With ....

Story Behind It ....

....

....

....

What was the experience like

What I learned ....

....

....

Experience Rating ⭐ ⭐ ⭐ ⭐ ⭐

#69

··
··

I Want to do this because ··
··

To Make This Happen I Need to ································
··

Time Frame ☐ now ☐ soon ☐ by the age of ···········

Date Completed ····················· Location ····················
Solo / With ··
Story Behind It ···
··
··
··

What was the experience like

What I learned ··
··
··

Experience Rating ⭐ ⭐ ⭐ ⭐ ⭐

#70

....

....

I Want to do this because ....

....

To Make This Happen I Need to ....

....

Time Frame ☐ now ☐ soon ☐ by the age of ....

Date Completed .... Location ....

Solo / With ....

Story Behind It ....

....

....

....

What was the experience like

What I learned ....

....

....

Experience Rating ⭐ ⭐ ⭐ ⭐ ⭐

#71

....

....

I want to do this because ....

....

To Make This Happen I Need to ....

....

Time Frame ☐ now ☐ soon ☐ by the age of ....

Date Completed .... Location ....

Solo / With ....

Story Behind It ....

....

....

....

What was the experience like

What I learned ....

....

....

Experience Rating ⭐ ⭐ ⭐ ⭐ ⭐

#72

....
....

I Want to do this because ....
....

To Make This Happen I Need to ....
....

Time Frame ☐ now ☐ soon ☐ by the age of ....

Date Completed .... Location ....
Solo / With ....
Story Behind It ....
....
....
....

What was the experience like

What I learned ....
....
....

Experience Rating ☆ ☆ ☆ ☆ ☆

#73

....

....

I want to do this because ....

....

To Make This Happen I Need to ....

....

Time Frame ☐ now ☐ soon ☐ by the age of ....

Date Completed .... Location ....

Solo / With ....

Story Behind It ....

....

....

....

What was the experience like

What I learned ....

....

....

Experience Rating ⭐ ⭐ ⭐ ⭐ ⭐

#74

....

....

I want to do this because ....

....

To Make This Happen I Need to ....

....

Time Frame ☐ now ☐ soon ☐ by the age of ....

Date Completed .... Location ....

Solo / With ....

Story Behind It ....

....

....

....

What was the experience like

What I learned ....

....

....

Experience Rating ☆ ☆ ☆ ☆ ☆

#75

....

....

I Want to do this because ....

....

To Make This Happen I Need to ....

....

Time Frame ☐ now ☐ soon ☐ by the age of ....

Date Completed .... Location ....

Solo / With ....

Story Behind It ....

....

....

....

What was the experience like

What I learned ....

....

....

Experience Rating ⭐ ⭐ ⭐ ⭐ ⭐

#76

....

....

I want to do this because ....

....

To Make This Happen I Need to ....

....

Time Frame ☐ now ☐ soon ☐ by the age of ....

Date Completed .... Location ....

Solo / With ....

Story Behind It ....

....

....

....

What was the experience like

What I learned ....

....

....

Experience Rating ☆ ☆ ☆ ☆ ☆

#77

....
....

I Want to do this because ....

....

To Make This Happen I Need to ....

....

Time Frame ☐ now ☐ soon ☐ by the age of ....

Date Completed .... Location ....

Solo / With ....

Story Behind It ....

....

....

....

What was the experience like

What I learned ....

....

....

Experience Rating ⭐ ⭐ ⭐ ⭐ ⭐

#78

I Want to do this because ....
....

To Make This Happen I Need to ....
....

Time Frame ☐ now ☐ soon ☐ by the age of ....

Date Completed .... Location ....
Solo / With ....
Story Behind It ....
....
....
....

What was the experience like

What I learned ....
....
....

Experience Rating ☆ ☆ ☆ ☆ ☆

#79

....

....

I Want to do this because ....

....

To Make This Happen I Need to ....

....

Time Frame ☐ now ☐ soon ☐ by the age of ....

Date Completed .... Location ....

Solo / With ....

Story Behind It ....

....

....

....

What was the experience like

What I learned ....

....

....

Experience Rating ⭐ ⭐ ⭐ ⭐ ⭐

#80

....

....

I Want to do this because ....

....

To Make This Happen I Need to ....

....

Time Frame ☐ now ☐ soon ☐ by the age of ....

Date Completed .... Location ....

Solo / With ....

Story Behind It ....

....

....

....

What was the experience like

What I learned ....

....

....

Experience Rating ☆ ☆ ☆ ☆ ☆

#81

....

....

I Want to do this because ....

....

To Make This Happen I Need to ....

....

Time Frame ☐ now ☐ soon ☐ by the age of ....

Date Completed .... Location ....

Solo / With ....

Story Behind It ....

....

....

....

What was the experience like

What I learned ....

....

....

Experience Rating ⭐ ⭐ ⭐ ⭐ ⭐

#82

....

....

I Want to do this because ....

....

To Make This Happen I Need to ....

....

Time Frame ☐ now ☐ soon ☐ by the age of ....

Date Completed .... Location ....

Solo / With ....

Story Behind It ....

....

....

....

What was the experience like

What I learned ....

....

....

Experience Rating ⭐ ⭐ ⭐ ⭐ ⭐

#83

....
....

I Want to do this because ....
....

To Make This Happen I Need to ....
....

Time Frame ☐ now ☐ soon ☐ by the age of ....

Date Completed .... Location ....
Solo / With ....
Story Behind It ....
....
....
....

What was the experience like

What I learned ....
....
....

Experience Rating ⭐ ⭐ ⭐ ⭐ ⭐

#84 ....
....

I Want to do this because ....

....

To Make This Happen I Need to ....

....

Time Frame ☐ now ☐ soon ☐ by the age of ....

Date Completed .... Location ....

Solo / With ....

Story Behind It ....

....

....

....

What was the experience like

What I learned ....

....

....

Experience Rating ⭐ ⭐ ⭐ ⭐ ⭐

#85

....

....

I want to do this because ....

....

To Make This Happen I Need to ....

....

Time Frame ☐ now ☐ soon ☐ by the age of ....

Date Completed .... Location ....

Solo / With ....

Story Behind It ....

....

....

....

What was the experience like

What I learned ....

....

....

Experience Rating ⭐ ⭐ ⭐ ⭐ ⭐

#86

....

....

I Want to do this because ....

....

To Make This Happen I Need to ....

....

Time Frame ☐ now ☐ soon ☐ by the age of ....

Date Completed .... Location ....

Solo / With ....

Story Behind It ....

....

....

....

What was the experience like

What I learned ....

....

....

Experience Rating ⭐ ⭐ ⭐ ⭐ ⭐

#87

....

....

I Want to do this because ....

....

To Make This Happen I Need to ....

....

Time Frame ☐ now ☐ soon ☐ by the age of ....

Date Completed .... Location ....

Solo / With ....

Story Behind It ....

....

....

....

What was the experience like

What I learned ....

....

Experience Rating ⭐ ⭐ ⭐ ⭐ ⭐

#88

....

....

I Want to do this because ....

....

To Make This Happen I Need to ....

....

Time Frame ☐ now ☐ soon ☐ by the age of ....

Date Completed .... Location ....

Solo / With ....

Story Behind It ....

....

....

....

What was the experience like

What I learned ....

....

....

Experience Rating ⭐ ⭐ ⭐ ⭐ ⭐

#89

....

....

I Want to do this because ....

....

To Make This Happen I Need to ....

....

Time Frame ☐ now ☐ soon ☐ by the age of ....

Date Completed .... Location ....

Solo / With ....

Story Behind It ....

....

....

....

What was the experience like

What I learned ....

....

....

Experience Rating ⭐ ⭐ ⭐ ⭐ ⭐

#90

··

··

I want to do this because ····································

···

To Make This Happen I Need to ···························

···

Time Frame ☐ now ☐ soon ☐ by the age of ···········

Date Completed ···················· Location ················

Solo / With ···

Story Behind It ···

···

···

···

What was the experience like

What I learned ···

···

···

Experience Rating ⭐ ⭐ ⭐ ⭐ ⭐

#91 ....
....

I Want to do this because ....
....

To Make This Happen I Need to ....
....

Time Frame ☐ now ☐ soon ☐ by the age of ....

Date Completed .... Location ....
Solo / With ....
Story Behind It ....
....
....
....

What was the experience like

What I learned ....
....
....

Experience Rating ⭐ ⭐ ⭐ ⭐ ⭐

#92

....

....

I want to do this because ....

....

To Make This Happen I Need to ....

....

Time Frame ☐ now ☐ soon ☐ by the age of ....

Date Completed .... Location ....

Solo / With ....

Story Behind It ....

....

....

....

What was the experience like

What I learned ....

....

....

Experience Rating ☆ ☆ ☆ ☆ ☆

#93 ....
....

I Want to do this because ....
....

To Make This Happen I Need to ....
....

Time Frame ☐ now ☐ soon ☐ by the age of ....

Date Completed .... Location ....
Solo / With ....
Story Behind It ....
....
....
....

What was the experience like

What I learned ....
....
....

Experience Rating ⭐ ⭐ ⭐ ⭐ ⭐

#94

....
....

I want to do this because ....
....

To Make This Happen I Need to ....
....

Time Frame ☐ now ☐ soon ☐ by the age of ....

Date Completed .... Location ....
Solo / With ....
Story Behind It ....
....
....
....

What was the experience like

What I learned ....
....
....

Experience Rating ☆ ☆ ☆ ☆ ☆

#95 ....
....

I Want to do this because ....
....

To Make This Happen I Need to ....
....

Time Frame ☐ now ☐ soon ☐ by the age of ....

Date Completed .... Location ....
Solo / With ....
Story Behind It ....
....
....
....

What was the experience like

What I learned ....
....
....

Experience Rating

#96

....
....

I want to do this because ....

....

To Make This Happen I Need to ....

....

Time Frame ☐ now ☐ soon ☐ by the age of ....

Date Completed .... Location ....

Solo / With ....

Story Behind It ....

....

....

....

What was the experience like

What I learned ....

....

....

Experience Rating ⭐ ⭐ ⭐ ⭐ ⭐

#97 ....
....

I Want to do this because ....
....

To Make This Happen I Need to ....
....

Time Frame ☐ now ☐ soon ☐ by the age of ....

Date Completed .... Location ....
Solo / With ....
Story Behind It ....
....
....
....

What was the experience like

What I learned ....
....
....

Experience Rating ⭐ ⭐ ⭐ ⭐ ⭐

#98 ....
....

I want to do this because ....
....

To Make This Happen I Need to ....
....

Time Frame ☐ now ☐ soon ☐ by the age of ....

Date Completed .... Location ....
Solo / With ....
Story Behind It ....
....
....
....

What was the experience like

What I learned ....
....
....

Experience Rating ☆ ☆ ☆ ☆ ☆

#99

....
....

I want to do this because ....
....

To Make This Happen I Need to ....
....

Time Frame ☐ now ☐ soon ☐ by the age of ....

Date Completed .... Location ....
Solo / With ....
Story Behind It ....
....
....
....

What was the experience like

What I learned ....
....
....

Experience Rating

#100 ....
....

I Want to do this because ....
....

To Make This Happen I Need to ....
....

Time Frame ☐ now ☐ soon ☐ by the age of ....

Date Completed .... Location ....
Solo / With ....
Story Behind It ....
....
....
....

What was the experience like

What I learned ....
....
....

Experience Rating ☆ ☆ ☆ ☆ ☆

CPSIA information can be obtained
at www.ICGtesting.com
Printed in the USA
BVHW050031230221
600801BV00008B/418